Walking Triptychs

Shanghai Poems

Ilya Gutner

Teaneck, New Jersey

Walking Triptychs ©2022 Ilya Gutner. All rights reserved. No part of this book may be used or reproduced in any manner whatsoever without written permission except in the case of brief quotations embodied in critical articles and reviews.

Published by Ben Yehuda Press
122 Ayers Court #1B
Teaneck, NJ 07666

http://www.BenYehudaPress.com

To subscribe to our monthly book club and support independent Jewish publishing, visit https://www.patreon.com/BenYehudaPress

Jewish Poetry Project #19   http://jpoetry.us

Ben Yehuda Press books may be purchased at a discount by synagogues, book clubs, and other institutions buying in bulk. For information, please email markets@BenYehudaPress.com

"The Duke of Meow" and "God's Bananas" first appeared in *Cough Syrup Magazine*, issue 3.
"God's good old China" first appeared in *The Cordite Review* (cordite.org.au).
"I take the keys, take money" first appeared at the *Big Windows Review* website.

ISBN13 978-1-953829-14-6

Library of Congress Cataloging-in-Publication Data

21 22 23 / 10 9 8 7 6 5 4 3 2 1 G2   20211031

Contents

Dedication vii
Letter to the Reader... viii
[Note of Conscience] ix

First Set 1

first triptych

α Try walking from the suburbs to the city 2
β A silence like the silence of the mind 3
γ Eating a duck egg in the street 4

My two kind angels 5

second triptych

α Poem about a raindrop 7
β Thoughts while reading Aristotle's Ethics 8
γ The cause of the tattoos 9

Thoughts at an intersection in Minhang 10

Second set 11

first triptych

α God's job in China 12
β God's bananas 14
γ God's good old China 16

second triptych

α I take the keys, take money 19
β The ship of clouds at dawn 20
γ An old fiddler has his fiddle 21

Walking in Shanghai 22

Third set 23

first triptych

α Confucius and the Duke of Meow 24
β Fish Silence Lake 27
γ At table with the Polish rabbis in Shanghaiz............................... 28

Jewish Saturday... 29

Second triptych

α Master Bilbo Baggins on a visit to Shanghai............................... 30
β The Muslims at the dormitory... 32
γ Hippie rabbi 33

Remembering Shanghai.. 35
Thinking about Gadamer and Plato 36

About the Author 37

Better to stand than to walk, to sit than to stand,
and best of all is lying down.
—Chinese saying.

Ilya Gutner

To my mother:
for her money.

Letter to the Reader

These are poems from when I walked about Shanghai and thought about the meaning of the Holocaust. Why did I think about the meaning of the Holocaust? That is answered by what brought me to China in the first place. What brought me to China? Only the encounter with the plain reality that in the West the Nazis really won, under a hundred different names. Theirs was not a unitary thought. Gathering my own thoughts in a unity, I came to the conclusion that it does not matter if they won or not. No evil had been done except if we forget the evil. Why do we forget the evil? Because if I forget the evil which is at the roots of my life, it is easier to think that the temporary pleasures and worries that my life is filled with, are important. So that I can go and love myself, and not like other people, under a hundred different names, forgetting the simple meaning of the one name I was born with: Human. To be human is to have inherited the Holocaust; and to pretend this does not matter, is to prefer the inheritance of something other than humanity to be my innate name. But in truth, this cannot be explained, only understood. So I do not know what need there could be for writing many words. I agree with the most fat and jolly rabbis: it is incumbent on us to rejoice, not in the spite of evil, but because evil is also in the world, and that is good, and very good that it should be this way. To remember the reality of evil, and to rejoice that all things should be so, is the true meaning of being Jewish; and that we Jews are those who do remember, and who would feel cheated if we had to live in a glass world as smooth and perfect as a bubble, is the reason why the Jews will go on in this world, and never disappear as long as it will stand. Who is this book addressed to, then? All those who have been confused in youth by the plurality of being and the unity of truth. It is my wish that this might be a guide along the way.

Sincerely and truly,
Light and laughter!
I.

November, 2019

Note of Conscience

If one fire is put out, or even if many fires and very great ones, few will think that from now there will be no more fires in existence; but when it comes to existential evil, we are all inclined to quarrel about words. No one has had such a welcome as I have in China; and in this book I have written my best words of praise for this country, which alone of all the countries of the world gave out legitimate, travel-worthy visas respected even by the Japanese, who even when the SS man came to Shanghai and ordered them to prepare a death camp, clicked their heels, said Hai! – (not Hail! but Hai! - since they were Japanese, and that is what one says in Japanese to such things) – and did nothing. The more so must I make my note of conscience here about the violations in Xinjiang. This is a new fire, of the same kind as the Holocaust, and that it has risen up on the other side of the globe, or that the direct victims of it are not Jews but Muslims, is only a quarrel about words in which it is our evil laziness of self that makes it easy to forget that once our neighbor's house starts burning, our own house is next. The signs of it are everywhere, even in Shanghai. An outdoor market closes down for maintenance and reopens a month later with all the goods again for sale and all the merchants there except the Uyghur with his big round flat-bread oven, so that you will not buy roast round naan-cakes anymore, unless if it should be a Han bread-maker puts an oven like that next to his steam furnace, having added this new skill as well to all he knows to do with flour and a flame. Go to the city center where four years ago you would be sold a great slice of a mountain cake, whether you will or nill, by the burly woman with her big knife, and you will not find this delicacy of the ancient Silk Road there any more: only clean-shaved businessmen and smooth-haired businesswomen walking past a big red sign that says, Sweep Away The Black Market And Destroy the Crooks! Or come go with me to try and rent a room in a communal apartment far from the city center, say, Pudong. (And when we say Pudong, you know we talk about the distance of Staten Island from the Bronx with both the strips of water that divide them from Manhattan.) Come, friend, let me introduce you to that nice young broker who was himself surprised, three years ago, to find that not all the apartments in his portfolio were suitable to be registered with the police for foreigners and people from Xinjiang. Ask him, as my friend and I asked, why not the people from Xinjiang, and you can hear his practiced answer: Muslims are dangerous. But then we asked what is dangerous about them, and the young man faltered briefly, evidently never having thought about this part himself, but then he came up with an answer, which I guess you will now hear from him in all of practiced confidence: They do not eat pork.

For eighty years, we have been saying that the bystander's silence is what gave power to the evildoer's hands. And for eighty years we have been exchanging, step by step, the binding nature of our social contract for material symbols of connection in society. And should I now publish a book merely in symbol of my connection with both East and West, and not do what a good and law-abiding citizen of the world must do whenever he sees a house catch on fire? Is a new world at hand? No, nothing is less new under the Sun, in God or man. Yes, it is incumbent on us to rejoice at the fact of evil. We must be glad, and laugh, and dance that it is not we who are doing evil. Because to do evil is its own punishment already in itself, but to make the evil-doers angry at us, then angry at themselves, and then have hope of change, is what it is to love our neighbor as ourselves and fear God above all; and that already is its own reward.

I.

October, 2021

First set

Work makes free.
—Written on the gates of Auschwitz.

Let no man corrupt you with philosophy.
—From the letters of the apostle Paul.

First triptych

α

Try walking from the suburbs to the city
at night all night unsure about the way
for thinking about things! Good stars of heaven,
stars of the Universe, by custom endless many,
in reason maybe none we seem to see,

let us think together, stars,
let us reach an answer
about the purpose of existence.

God made a German clock one day
mastering his own world's laws of nature:
its gears the stars, morality its motion.

>   Walking from Minhang District
> my first spring of acquaintance with the noble doctrine
>   of the categorical imperative.

β

A silence like the silence of the mind!
I ride a horse of air, good people,
in my right hand a beam of sunshine,
on my shield a broken burning heart. Behold,
forgetting streets, I make the mud-paths mine!

In the vegetable gardens in Shanghai
the mud kissed my invading shoes,
the dragon of white smoke permitting.

Over that way is the coking plant:
there the dragon lives. In my heart,
here, the illness which you call Psychosis.

      Walking in Minhang
  down the mudpaths my feet hungered for
        walking in Manhattan.

γ

Husband and a wife
and a dumpling stand:
smiling all day long
because work is happiness.
Working all day long.

But a black-eyed daughter lives in England
where these dumplings and these pickled eggs
add up to a young woman's independence.

I, too, have a black-eyed daughter,
wants to go alone to England
to be there alone without me.

      Eating a duck egg in the street
I think about
      the dignity of art above the artist.

My two kind angels

Not women and not children nor old beggars
and not stray dogs, invisible not shapeless
because in the imagination you can see them clearly
where we shape images of how things seem.

Angels are God's messengers in many shapes:
they speak his will and run his errands
because without this God would not be God
as love is not itself without the letters.

I do not speak a cushioned softness
out of the pink-walled womb of doing nothing:
the Lord of Hosts must have his armies
and that is a great work for the imagination.

The night angel is fat with sides of flesh
like the laughing Buddha and the Friar
Chaucer went to Canterbury with,
the one who said his *In principio* so sweet
that even I was charmed by the sly rascal.

Sometimes the night angel is a turtle
clumsy in its shell with feet of stone:
feet of stone carved round with ancient words
clumsy on a shell carved round with stone.

I leave the window open my hand's breadth
drawing the curtain against the breath of the night wind
and the night angel squats square on my chest
    pushing away nightmares
    and excess hours of sleep
    and tells me about God
like an old Sumo wrestler telling stories
of his first monastery to a sleeping child.

The morning angel is a thief of time
shaped like a spoiled child's smile
with a cat's tail and a wild ox's eyes:
he sneaks in through locked doors

>   on feet that look like worms,
> worms worrying into each word they find,
>   being come to steal your concentration
> when you have steeled yourself to change your life by work.

If you sit about and ask him why he does this
he will reason with you like the black monk in the story
until you find that to be focused is too vulgar
for a man of your incredible abilities
to sit around doing just one thing all day.

The only thing to do about the morning angel
    if you do want to do work,
to do work and not to think about the good of working
    but without the work itself, is to
    give the lazy rascal infinite small chores
chasing him about with mop and laundry basket
till he leaves you like a child in tears
who came to play and was not wanted.

From this you can see
that the night angel is a help
whereas the morning angel is a hindrance.

Second triptych

α Poem about a raindrop

Escaping God's severity is nonsense.
Vanity to seek a gentle god.
You can be good and better and deserve
 therefore to witness mute with awe
  the awful wonders of the Lord.

A raindrop from a branch in the chill fog
struck my forehead like a finger's tap
as I went muttering these verses in the street
 and I was silent then
  as one ashamed of dinner at an egg-cake cart.

Was Job more guilty or am I
that the Lord owes answers to my curiosity,
my shallow longing for a word or two
 by which to understand
  what a life's seeking but approximates?

β

He who sets his mind to learn
sits down at the edge of being
where there is nothing there as yet
and matter waits for a new pattern,
a teenage girl at a tattoo parlor.

How can shapeless matter
be a teenage girl
at a tattoo parlor?

And if there is nothing there as yet
how can there be matter there at all?
Questions I hear asked me by the people.

   Thoughts while reading Aristotle's Ethics
  at a Chinese restaurant in China
    where I am stared at.

γ The cause of the tattoos

Moses is the memory of a migration
when they went forth in their thousands
and their tens of thousands, going forth,
a sociological phenomenon, and that means simply
what rests without an explanation on the Earth.

In the camps the Jews were also numbered
in the books of records and the wrist,
on the wrist where it became a sign
to remember walking on the way and sitting
and to teach your children when they ask.

Jews, Gypsies, Communists and beggars,
the Jehovah's Witnesses and the insane,
queer male homosexuals and plain ones,
thieves, fools, strangers, children without eyes,
shrinks, bawds, prostitutes, autistic children, pastors.

The numbers made it seem objective, like a science,
and quieted the conscience of the killers. Try it:
go number what you do because you do it,
not asking why you do it. Two and two
into the ark, one by one the gas chamber.

Green scarves round Arthur's Table;
word Nigger in the projects;
and now to mark uniquely,
to mark a body beautiful,
a body beautiful and young, -

Let there be symbols
of its passing beauty
on the young flesh
by each deserving lover
remembered till life's end.

Thoughts at an intersection in Minhang

Broken concentration is a step in sin.
Poets lean in into things because they are near-sighted.
Philosophers step back because they are not poets.
And that is all there is to that.

The cup's reflection shows in the glass door
my glasses are becoming useless;
the Suzhou River keeps on flowing:
and that is all there is to that.

I have a fear my three baked sweet potatoes
you will attribute to my acting strangely
and speaking strangely all my poetry
and that is all there is to that.

Second set

If God lived on earth, people would break His windows.
—Jewish saying.

First triptych

α God's job in China

Only one thing not good about the poetry of Ezra Pound:
the learned author is a Fascist bag of scum.
That was the Lord's last editorial decision
for the Sun Times before God left the States for good
for Shanghai, China. Why Shanghai? Because
this is the only city in the world
which took in Jewish refugees
on real, legitimate, respected visas even in the face
of the plain fact of occupation by the Japanese
who somehow did not have the face,
having the city in their hand, to kill the refugees
who came on visa from the last Confucian scholar-bureaucrat,
the famous special envoy to Berlin,
in those days when even New York turned away the Children's Ark
with words not on the torch of Lady Liberty,
in those long years when Pound was busy broadcasting his broadcasts
in Italy in English all about the kike;
and difficult good deeds do have to go for something with the Lord.
If the Lord God will not remember stubborn righteousness, who will?

So now God lives in China, in Shanghai.
His address is not easy to explain in English.
You really have to go to understand.
First God lived in Putuo
making Chinese steam buns but
he got tired explaining to the people
what it was he had against the using of the pig for meat.
The more you say the less they understand!

Then God moved to Minhang and there he went to work
at the new chemical plant, back in the eighties,
or maybe seventies (this part of the chronicle is dark),
where he worked peacefully as the day-watch security guard,
watching nothing happen
for almost thirty years on end
until he even got into the taste
of eating three pork buns for breakfast, three rice meals a day,
drinking white alcohol, riding a scooter, chatting on QQ,

playing Mahjong with his three friends on Friday nights for money
and studying in his time off from all these things
the Book of Tao and the I-Ching.
But then they found out he was into Falun Gong,
sent goons to break his windows, killed his cat
and bullied him at work with nasty looks and silence till he left.

Now the Lord lives in New Pudong District
half-way on the way to Disney Resort,
like Chaucer back from Canterbury at the Inn,
in one of those old houses no one wants, works
as something like a farmer, keeps a dog,
is friends with Liu Shaoqi the ghost
and does not own a phone.

Walking Triptychs

β God's bananas

Once God had a friend and all was fine.
They ate fish and chicken Friday nights,
went out on a walk on Saturdays,
gossiped all week long about the locals in Shanghai
and made plans to move to Greece
because there is too much news in Israel.

Then one day they tried to get a travel visa to the States.
Can any normal person have been friends with God?
Reason for rejection 214:
Suspected intention to immigrate.
God got angry:
God is God but God's friend is just a friend!
Who said it would be easy to be friends with God?

So the Lord called Moses for a loan of 700 Chinese dollars,
took a neighbor's pushcart, bought three bags of salted cookies
and a bag of green bananas,
took these to the intersection south of Hua Peng Road
and then went away because he was too angry to have patience
even to try changing his own life by going into business.

I was also angry at my friend today.
So I went on a long walk along Gao Qing
out to where they have the vegetable fields
one can stroll around and no one asks you why.
That was where I saw the cart with the bananas
and a city-uncle type sitting on a striped cement road divider
playing with his screen phone
like an angel with a fragment of the Ten Commandments.

Each time I pointed to the green bananas
he raised a long flat finger straight up to the sky and smiled so knowingly
that even I had to understand at last:
these are the bananas of the living God!
I thought he meant a dollar so I plucked off two,
a pair of green bananas,
and when the truth flashed upon me as I reached into my pocket for the cash
I would have put down four coins for the Lord but my hand put down only three.

I heard a sound of laughter as I walked away but I am used to being laughed at.
And I ate the bananas walking around the vegetable paths.

My friend, my friend, I did not even bring you God's bananas!

γ God's good old China

Everywhere you go is walking under heaven.
In those ruins east of Pusan Road
where the Shanghainese had homes before the Chinese Dream,
in that block of broken houses and farm fields run wild
locked in by that white-washed propaganda-picture wall,
there God lives on Earth in China,
having left the West for good when finally it got to him
that they still say what they still say:
If God lived on earth, people would break His windows.

And where is an almighty God to live if not on Earth?
What, out in outer space?
Shows how much you people love him!

So God went to live with the good old
domesticated and heartbroken Chinese ghosts and devils
and there God rented out a home
from the Howling Ghost Real Estate Agency,
a good brick-plaster kind of home
with a second-story balcony and all
and a big vegetable patch outside
to putter in about late evenings after work,
last in line nearest the corner with the security booth to the right
as you come walking from the east,
and in the booth a guard,
guarding by staring at his screen phone day and night,
to guard the ghosts and devils from themselves
who live in that long line of growling, moaning, doorless homes
windowless and full of shapeless rubbish
and dark, oy, when has it ever been so dark
except in the beginning, when the earth was void,
as they say in the book, and shapeless and the spirit of God
moved upon the surface of the deep?

Well, that was in the book, but in real life, a house,
white Honda in the mud outside,
that strange booth with the black-shirt guard inside
installed in symbol of the senselessness of the primeval chaos
by the Bodhisattva who is boss of Howling Ghost,
and an unbarking St. Bernard dog running back and forth along the river
mysteriously like the spirit of God upon the waters.

This is how God lives now in a place
where at least they will not break his windows, where
when curious folks, strangers to the place, come stumbling in the heaps
of that old once-important rubbish still important to itself,
he goes out on his Chinese motor scooter to investigate.

A balding short old village-uncle type
you will not meet much off the mainland,
beer paunch, open black polo shirt
and friendly smile as easy to mistake for a policeman's
uncomfortable tricks as he himself for a detective
in his black polo shirt with the big rhombus on the left side of the chest
which looks like a police badge in the dark.

And when he offers you a smoke
remember that we meet God's face in every stranger,
remember and do not do as I did.
I with my fear
that every stranger works for the police.

Do not say: No need.
Just accept.

It is wrong to blame God for the Holocaust
and foolishness to argue smart-phone thoughts
and I feel hopeless on my mother's birthday
because she is the one who pays my debts.

Death is God's gift to his Creation,
which rhymed with Debt in Falstaff's day. One day
I will fall into the Suzhou River
while listening to God talk about himself.

The Lord is an old Jewish tailor
sometimes mistakes a man's suit for boy's clothing
and cuts the infinite like discount fabric
to give you just the thing he made. Oy vey!

Go reason with him if you got the patience!
A door will always open to distract you.
A box of children's vitamins will tell you
about as much as all I have to say.

Second triptych

α

I take the keys, take money,
close the door, cross the tracks
where trains approach the city's heart
and then I cross the bridge
and go down to the river.

Green plant floating
under drizzling rain.
Good-bye, my friend.

The way back up
not burdened by you
is steeper than before.

      Giving proper funeral
to the green plant with brown leaves
      on my balcony.

β

The ship of clouds at dawn
is known to every bird's nest
still left by my mother's house
on Staten Island since the flood
that changed New York this decade.

A small black cat
with white paws stalks
at my low window.

All this is rather difficult to put in words
the more that I would rather have said nothing
than talk to people here. But in a word: Good-bye.

    Considering the past
on my three trips back home
    before the future.

γ

An old fiddler has his fiddle,
an old baker has his bread:
I sit outside the local eatery
listening to minor local bullies eat
their four small dishes, drinking beer.

They are drinking beer and I am drinking.
Little did I think ten years ago beer
an inspired beverage of wisdom worth the gods!

Four more men stumble by: one angry
in the local dialect keeps turning back,
a dull drunken flash of gambler's indignation.

      Watching young men angry at their bosses
  and old men at their partners
      while growing paper mushrooms at a restaurant.

Walking in Shanghai

I have no one who will hear my sadness
and none will listen to me speak my heart
here in the city of the workers' Dawn,
the famous City on the Sea.

If I address myself to God
my voice stops short: I am unclean.
If I address myself to people
the voice sounds false with which I speak.

To whom my sadness
and to whom my loneliness?
Surely I have spoken to my notebooks
and they have answered me with silence
and then they answered me with tongues of flame.

For fearing others than the Lord
thrown down from Sinai I walk thus shattered,
a limping fool as frightened of myself
as dogs and children are of such a stranger:

A stranger walking in the field of stars!

Third set

$$\alpha = \frac{M\kappa}{4\pi^2}$$
—Einstein's formula for the shape of the Universe, 1921 Princeton Lectures, Lecture 4.

"The Chinese tolerated us. Yeah! They tolerated us!"
—Video recording at the Jewish Refugees' Museum in Shanghai.

"Three Squeaks"
—Name of a traditional Chinese dish, which consists of using chopsticks to pick up live suckling mice, dipping them alive in soy sauce and then swallowing them whole.

First triptych

α Confucius and the Duke of Meow

Whoever tells you making poetry is making love
is obviously lying about money instruments
but there is something there alike.
No, not that on an empty stomach you do neither well
because Osip Mandelstam was hungry all the three years in Voronezh
and yet there is his poem about the evil stars and picture by Rembrandt,
the poem about the snow-finch and the poem about Dante's
athletic flying circles lost
in the blue palate of the sky,
and no one has made better poetry than that, or ever will,
though there be plenty well-fed poets in all ages.

No, no, and no, not that, good people.
But to eat is happiness, you see,
and you will find no poets who do not like having things to eat;
and not too many lovers, I believe.

Now one night Confucius ate too many steam buns,
the ones with the diced pork and leeks, and drank a cup too much
of the rice wine with warm bamboo cakes on the side
(said to go well together, all three things being white:
white buns, white cakes, white wine)
and even sages are susceptible to happiness
so he went straight to bed and even kissed his wife
exactly 81 times,
which is the Most Male Number (9 x 9)
and fell asleep to dream about the Duke of Chow.

Poor Confucius! No one ever told him time is curved
(nor is it probable that he would understand)
so that in short the Duke of Chow that visited his dreams,
in the old orthography before he became Duke of Zhou in pinyin,
to tell him how the rituals were conducted in the olden days,
around the end of the Stone Age, the really olden days,
is the white kitten with the black and grey like a small tiger's stripes
all round his back, under his eyes and on his ears
my friend picked up this Summer from the cardboard box
at the entrance to our building here in Pudong

where he was left to die
back in those days before the big green tree outside
had half its branches lopped off like a Russian convict
back in the Russia of the Tsars
because it blocked somebody's first-floor light.

Cat Duke we called him, Duke of Meow:
we were looking for a tomcat
for our other kitten to be paired with for when she grew up
and Duke Cat is the normal way to say a tomcat in the standard dialect.
And so Cat Duke, the Duke of Meow.

In the first week we found that he had an infected paw:
he bore up manfully under the torture of my treatment
and lost a claw, which I regretted more than he.
In the first month he taught me courage to start reading Darwin.
In the third month the chutzpah to start reading Einstein
without two plus signs of a mathematics in my hand.
In the fourth month I let him go
because he made me angry with his noisy play at night.
And now I see him in my dreams.

But time is curved and he is not to find
when I look around the neighborhood in vain
knocking with a metal chopstick on a glass jar,
like a Romantic ballad walking round at night
with a glass jar and metal chopstick in my hands, and in my heart regret,
remembering my annoyance at my friend all Summer long
while she made herself busy teaching the cats this signal to receive their meat:
gong-gong-gong-twang-gong-gong-twang-twang!
And where is Plato's dignity in language?

But time is curved and space is not Euclidean,
and what Confucius woke up to remember as the Duke of Chow,
giving the old sage advice on how to run things well
(to run things really well,
so nothing new would ever, ever, ever happen,
because only the bored can ever want new things to happen
and no one can be bored who has a pair of balls)
is actually my pet the Duke of Meow.

But only that one night
after the Three White Things and the Dragon Change of Kisses
did Confucius see the cat as is
and did not see it differently upon awaking.
And that is why in Book One of the Analects
Confucius says:

A gentleman does not need to be filled with eating.

If I miss my cat, then so I do.
That is my own business. I only meant to tell you why
life in China is so much like living in a land of cats
with cat morality, cat loves, cat self-respect.

β Fish Silence Lake

By a man-made lake near Zhongshan Park
(everything is man-made under heaven)
you can meet with Sun Yat-sen
who is now the body of a breeze
bringing quiet explanations
to whoever sits there with a quiet mind.
But I do not want to praise this country.
I have said enough to praise this country.
Now I want to speak about the fish.

The fish pluck up with their mouths at the water's face
like kisses on the surface of the deep:
black Li, red Li, more black Li than the red,
narrow all lengthwise like the lake-weeds they swim in among
and silent, very silent, like the clouds among the weeds.
Kissing the water they invert the raindrops
which must not come down from a silent sky
by the eternal ordinance of nature
that when it rains there is a sound of raining
and water does not come down from a silent sky.

Then the wind comes to explain:

You sit here with your friend confessing love
forgetting for the minute all the eyes that stare,
those eyes that keep on staring at their own new China
as if a foreigner had been a walking fish,
a foreigner who walks with one of the Chinese,
you sit here by the lake among the fish
and in the silence of the lake hear the reflected silence
of ancient ages with their own new times
of ancient ages that passed by just so
in noise and silence, silence made of noise.

γ At table with the Polish rabbis in Shanghai

How filled I am with Sun's light and the stars!
I glory now like a fanatic at his teacher's execution,
fear and jubilation, wine and water in my broken thoughts
to see these huge new buildings rising in the dark
from where the cultivated earth lay last year wisely growing
and will again when time comes to respect old things.

Past burns with truth
as the meat offerings
burned with the good white fat at
       God's hard altar.

And what we call
our modern age ascends
smoke of burnt offerings at Aaron's hand
       by simple burning.

The truth burns unconsumed
like the crumb miracles
at table with the rabbis when
       their time was.

Then no one bothered counting when and how.
Because, God being present, what is absent then?
Sifting the ashes at the death camps, Time,
God's angel of necessity, found the old crumbs
refined to gold of sinless confidence upon the Earth.

Jewish Saturday

Considering all things as they most are,
God is to be feared, not language
and fear of words betokens secret guilt.

I gather emptiness into my hand
to make a world of truth
out of a world of silence.

Spilling the blood of Sabbath-days
in ink and smart-phone data
I feed the Chinese language
   teaching it to eat.

And that is why
you hear me laughing
in a fake voice
about the holy things.

Second triptych

α Master Bilbo Baggins on a visit to Shanghai

> "If the hobbits were an allegory for the Jews and the Ring for the atom bomb, then Sauron would have enslaved the hobbits and used the Ring to win the war."
> —Tolkien's preface to the Lord of the Rings, explaining his distaste for allegory.

> "The mandarin Wan-mao-in, the Chinese Chancellor of the Exchequer, took it into his head one day to lay before the Son of Heaven a proposal that secretly aimed at converting the *assignats* of the empire into convertible bank notes. The Assignats Committee, in its report of April, 1854, gives him a severe snubbing. Whether he also received the traditional drubbing with bamboos is not stated."
> —Marx, *Capital* part 1 chapter 3 section 3c, in a footnote.

If only it was all so simple
that the Chinese were industrious little hobbits, nice and tame:
for one they are not nice
and for another not what one calls tame!
These were the words poor master Baggins was about to say
to his friends Oin, Gloin, Balin, Dwalin and Bombur
waiting at the bus station at Long Cao
watching the people push and push and push
when Gandalf finally came back
with their seventh breakfast
from the egg-cake, rolled-rice, roast-cake and steamed-bun stands
across the busy, busy, busy street.
Hullo! And this is what one calls a suburb!

Then they stood there waiting for their bus to come,
the dwarves sweating in their hoods
and frowning all their eye-brows all at once
till Dwalin could not take it and he said:
In all this famous city on the sea
(may it never run dry of the precious old jade we provide to trade in!)
in all this famous city there is not one beard,
it seems, except for ours for all the people all to look at!

Oh, do not mention it, said Gandalf, chewing on a bun:
I have lived here fifty years now, and
the one thing they have never done yet was stop staring.
I even had a project once I drafted for the city council
to have the sidewalks planted on each side with trees,
with walls of trees just like a corridor
with lanterns hanging in the branches and the sidewalk raised
to make room for the roots.
I even showed them selfies of myself from Mirkwood!
The reason they refused was because of their spy cameras:
they were afraid bad people would do bad things
if they were not continually being watched;
but in my Mirkwood Corridors their cameras would need
the help of magic not to have blind spots. I said,
What magic, just chop a few heads right off at the start!
But they just fiddled with their papers
and said that is a feudal and reactionary way of thought.

β

The Muslims at the dormitory
gave two packs of milk
to me today this morning;
and since the morning I
drink coffee all day long.

I am reading Mo Yan's book about the Sorghum
in Chinese, and about China know enough now, I,
to know what about the Sorghum makes it red.

The author need not lie about the past:
the past is in the past. But that
teaches me not to think about the past.

      Questioning the future
in the middle of my fourth year living here
      in mainland China.

γ Hippie rabbi

Who is that said never to remember anything
or you start missing everyone like something bad?
It makes no difference, I suppose,
only it would be nice to know.
Yes, you know, nice,
if you do know
and if you still remember what nice is
as I try to remember now and then
how once I met the hippie rabbi by the Wailing Wall.

What was I doing in Jerusalem?
Loafing, you know.
Like the Chinese say, just rubbing fish.
You know, I was not twenty-two.
It was less than three years since I found out that there is a God.
Man, I was young.

He walks up to me and says:
You have some chutzpah wearing a bandana to the Wailing Wall!
Then took out his wallet and gave me a card,
and he says:
Come for dinner on Shabbat.
Just an ordinary-looking rabbi.
The round black hat and big white beard and all.

Who thought I would remember him in China
when of the inclination of my own good will
I started praying thrice a day in Greek
at dawn, past noon, and in the evening
after the darkness settles on the city
where the white smog is like a fish at dawn
and I put a bandana on to pray
which I picked off a bush
to decorate my room with for Shabbat?

He spread his vegetable meal in pride of self
before me and the friends I brought from the Yeshiva
who all agreed variety improves a Friday night.
He told us one's own righteousness comes first

so first put food in your own plate
then pass it to your neighbor,
since food on Friday is a blessing
and never mind the grammar which you know.

He told us how he sat in Central Park
back in the Sixties and the people all came out
like Christians to the river
to sit by him and feel his aura and be healed.
And then he went to India to be a Yogi.
But one day there came to him three cripples,
who woke up in the Buddhist Scriptures just that morning and came out
to tempt,
and so he cured them with his aura,
cured their bodies of the body's ill
but as they walked away he saw their souls:
their souls were ugly and were limping crookedly
which was not so before the bodies had been healed.

And that is how the old reverse-Siddhartha
came back to the West, became a rabbi
and came in course of time to live there by the Wailing Wall
in the Old City in Jerusalem,
which is where he met me in his loneliness,
to make his way to China in this poem.

Where I still have the chutzpah to believe
that all this happened so that I might learn to pray in Greek:
the wise men schlep to bring gifts from the East,
they bring back hope and go again and do not cease.

Remembering Shanghai

Takes no time to know infinity.
God exists, so death is real as well.
I saw a plastic bag on a green bush
at night and picked it up: what for?

That plastic bag drew my attention like
a peasant selling baked potatoes in the street
and like the waters in the river when
the people fish in it at night.

Why now, why now, why now? Why here as well
but answer me in order as I ask
or I will be confused: this inspired state
of false comparisons inhibits truth.

Thinking about Gadamer and Plato,
Kant's categorical imperative, the Nazis
and the Jews, Palestine and
Israel and this disgusting dormitory
and a raindrop struck me.

China is at the world's end.
I am also here in China.
This is a wonder to consider.

Let me consider it in wisdom, wisdom.
Wisdom is taught by the falling rain,
by a single rain drop's sudden fall.

    Another poem
  about another raindrop
      in Shanghai.

About the Author

Ilya Gutner lives with his wife, their variable set of cats, the village dogs that come scraping at the door and the village rain that comes knocking at the window, in a farmer's backshed in a village on the disappearing city outskirts of Shanghai; grumbles day and night about the daily and the nightly rumble from the construction site next door; and is a student of philosophy.

www.ingramcontent.com/pod-product-compliance
Lightning Source LLC
LaVergne TN
LVHW041347080426
835512LV00006B/652